S0-BLO-174

Bride

Debra Keller

Illustrated by

Diane Hobbing

Ariel Books

**Andrews McMeel
Publishing**

Kansas City

Bride

ISBN: 0-7407-3364-8
Library of Congress Catalog Card Number:
2002111882

Bride

Introduction

Maybe you've **dreamed** about being a bride since you were little, or maybe it's a position you swore you'd never **find yourself** in, but now *that you're here, embrace it! It's one of the most important roles of* your life.

In any wedding, *no matter how big or how small, whether it's traditional or unique, the bride is the main attraction. She's the center of the* celebration, *a reminder of love, a symbol of* hope and happiness.

B r i d e

There are countless ways to be a **bride** and in this book you'll discover some of them. Perhaps you'll find yourself in its pages, or maybe it will **spark** an idea or two. Read on, fear not, and congratulations! The **journey** of your lifetime is about to **begin.**

I love you, not

for what you are,

Bride

but for what I

am when I am with

you.

—Roy Croft

11

Let Them Eat Cake

When Queen Elizabeth married Prince Phillip in 1947, she had nine wedding cakes made. The one she cut at her reception was nine feet tall and weighed five hundred pounds.

On Your Left, Please

*M*ost brides stand
to the left of the
groom, a tradition
that dates back to
pagan times when

"marriage by capture" *was the common way to wed. A groom used to steal his bride from her family, so he needed his sword hand (usually the right) free for defense.*

I know some **good** marriages—marriages where both people are just trying to get through their days by **helping** each other, being good to each other.

—*Erica Jong*

Though you

be *two*

that love,

B r i d e

let there be one

heart

between you.

–Italian proverb

Longer Than a Locomotive

The longest wedding dress train *was 670 feet. It was worn by Hege Lorence in Norway in 1996 and required 186 bridesmaids and page boys to carry it.*

From every human being there rises a light that reaches straight to heaven, and when two souls that are destined to be together find each other, the streams of light flow together and a single brighter light goes forth from that united being.

—Ba'al Shem Tov

Bride

What's the **secret** of a happy marriage? Call me a **romantic** if you want, but for me, the answer is the same simple, **beautiful** idea that has been making relationships work for thousands of years: **separate bathrooms.**

—Dave Barry

Invitation

Sealed With a Kiss

In early Roman times, a contract was bound with a kiss. No marriage was valid without one.

We share pretty much everything, except for, you know, dresses.

–Kate Hudson,
on her husband Chris Robinson

27

Dress Rehearsal

Girls, if they're typical, begin rehears-ing for their wedding when they're about four years old. Many dress up like brides and toddle down the aisle . . . without a groom, however.

Bride

That's the Way They All Became . . .

*W*hen Carol Martin married Mike Brady on the TV sitcom The Brady Bunch, *their combined six kids, two pets, and housekeeper, Alice, all but ruined the ceremony.*

29

We are partners— in public and in private.

—Queen Rania of Jordan,
on her marriage to King Abdullah

Bride

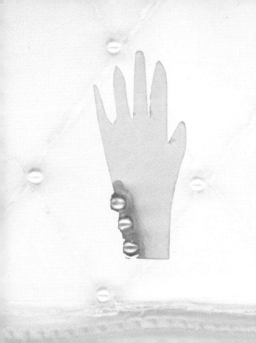

Bridal Reign

The difference between being a **bride** *and being a* **queen** *is the number of people under your rule.*

Look
for a sweet
person.

B r i d e

Forget rich.

—Estée Lauder,
on choosing a spouse

Romantic Wedding Movies to Watch

Father of the Bride

Four Weddings and a Funeral

Runaway Bride

My Best Friend's Wedding

Bride

Philadelphia Story

The Graduate

Muriel's Wedding

It Happened One Night

Like Water for Chocolate

The Wedding Singer

A successful
marriage
requires
falling in love
many times,

B r i d e

always with
the same
person.

–*Mignon McLaughlin*

39

$\mathcal{L}$ove means the body, the soul,

the life, the entire being. We feel love

as we feel the warmth of our blood,

we breathe love as we breathe air,

we hold it in ourselves as we hold our

thoughts. Nothing more exists for us.

–Guy de Maupassant

B r i d e

The secret to a good marriage
is not having a TV in the bedroom.

–Kim Cattrall

Honeymoon Sleep-In

Yoko Ono married John Lennon in 1969, a time when sit-ins were popular. They honeymooned in Amsterdam, where they spent seven days in bed together, talking to reporters and promoting world peace.

B r i d e

Something (Very) Old

When Princess Anne married in 1973, her "something old" was a sprig of myrtle in her bridal bouquet. It was grown from the myrtle Queen Victoria carried down the aisle in 1840.

If Traditions R Not 4 U

*A*dventurous brides are dumping tradition in favor of weddings with flair. Here are a few popular themes:

At a ski resort . . . on the slopes

At a southern plantation, in period dress

On horseback

B r i d e

Skydiving (the bride wearing a white jumpsuit, of course)

In a hot-air balloon

On a roller coaster

Rock climbing

Scuba diving

In a big league ballpark

In a medieval forest (with Merlin as minister)

In ancient Egypt

*P*eople are always asking couples whose **marriage** has endured at least a quarter of a century for their **secret** for success. Actually, it is no secret at all. I am a forgiving woman. Long ago, I forgave my husband for not being Paul Newman.

—Erma Bombeck

Bride

Seaxiness wears thin after a while and beauty fades, but to be **married** to a man who makes you **laugh** every day, ah, now that's a real treat.

–*Joanne Woodward,*
on her husband Paul Newman

. . . *t*hey have a **deep** friendship and **love** for each other. But it's realistic, not sort of kissing around ridiculously and pretending everything's great and not dealing with all the ups and downs of a forty-year marriage. I **cherish** that. I'm so **glad** I have that to hold up.

—Nicole Kidman,
on her parents' marriage

49

My mom once said, "Honey, you should marry a rich man." I said, "Mom, I am a **rich** man."

—Cher

Bride

*H*e's **nutty**—he will do anything on earth to make me laugh.

–Jill Goodacre,
on her husband Harry Connick Jr.

Jumping

the Broom

any African-American brides "jump the broom" into marriage. It's a custom that dates back to before the Civil War, when slaves were denied legal rights and would marry by jumping over a broom together.

I married the first man I ever kissed. When I tell this to my children they just about throw up.

—*Barbara Bush*

B r i d e

My grandmother says that the **secret** to marriage is "Don't go to bed angry." She's been **awake** since 1936.

—*Wendy Liebman*

Madonna's Gift Wrap

When Madonna wed Guy Ritchie in 2000, the Reverend Susan Brown officiated. Reverend Brown gave the couple two rolls of toilet paper as a wedding gift because they're "long and strong, like their marriage will be."

$\mathcal{M}$arriage is not a ritual or an end. It is a long, intricate, intimate **dance** together and nothing matters more than your own **sense** of balance and your choice of partner.

—*Amy Bloom*

A Rose Is a Rose Is a Symbol of Love

According to the language of flowers, a bride's bouquet can speak volumes:

Baby's breath–fertility

Carnation–fidelity

Forsythia–anticipation

Gardenia—joy

Lily of the valley—devotion

Marigold—passion

Myrtle—luck

Orange blossoms—happiness

Sweet pea—pleasure

White lilac—innocence

$\mathcal{N}$o two

Beings ever

come together

for the

benefit of only

one.

–*Elia Wise*

B r i d e

$\mathcal{L}$ove in all its
forms can still grab
you and make you
roll the dice.

—*Amy Bloom*

The King of Weddings

If you've always dreamed of a royal wedding, you can be married by the king himself. At the Viva Las Vegas wedding chapel, Elvis presides. Choose from Hound Dog *Elvis,* Blue Hawaii *Elvis, or an Elvis from the jump-suited later years.*

B r i d e

Never Say Never

The oldest bride on record is Minnie Monroe. She was 102 when she married her beau, 83-year-old Dudley Reid.

$\mathcal{N}$othing in life is as good as marriage of true minds between man and woman. As good? It is life itself.

—Pearl S. Buck

Bride

*I*t took great **courage** to ask a beautiful young woman to marry me. Believe me, it is **easier** to play the whole of *Petrushka* on the piano.

—Arthur Rubinstein

Five of the Most Popular Songs for Walking Down the Aisle

"Bridal Chorus (Here Comes the Bride)" from Lohengrin (Wagner)

"Canon in D" (Pachelbel)

B r i d e

"Water Music" (Handel)

"What a Wonderful World" (Louis
Armstrong)

"I Can't Help Falling in Love" (Elvis
Presley)

I think men who have a **pierced** ear are better prepared for **marriage.** They've experienced pain and bought jewelry.

—*Rita Rudner*

B r i d e

For most of us, **marriage** is a strange and necessary fire, a red-hot light toward which we moths cannot keep ourselves from flying.

—*Vince Passaro*

Five of the Most Popular Songs for a Bride's First Dance

"Unforgettable" (Nat King Cole)

"From This Moment On" (Shania Twain)

B r i d e

"I Got You Babe" *(Sonny and Cher)*

"When a Man Loves a Woman" *(Percy Sledge)*

"At Last" *(Etta James)*

$\mathcal{W}$hen
the **wedding**
march sounds the
resolute approach, the clock
no longer ticks, it tolls the
hour. . . . The figures in the aisle
are no longer individuals. They
symbolize the human race.

–Anne Morrow Lindbergh

Love is every-

thing it's cracked up to be....

It really is worth fighting for,

being brave for, risking

everything for.

—*Erica Jong*

Five of the Most Popular Songs for a Bride's Dance with Her Dad

"My Girl" (The Temptations)

"My Dad" (Paul Petersen)

"Thank Heaven for Little Girls" (Gigi)

B r i d e

"A Song for My Daughter" (Mikki Verrick)

"Daddy's Little Girl" (Kippi Branon)

L♥ve,

Bride

like **_truth,_** is the unassailable defense.

—Diane Ackerman

*Book design and
composition by
Diane Hobbing of*
Snap-Haus Graphics
in Dumont, NJ